Super Simple Scroll Saw Clocks

by
John A. Nelson

Fox Chapel Publishing Co., Inc.
1970 Broad Street
East Petersburg, PA 17520

John Nelson and other scrollers throughout the country have teamed up with Fox Chapel Publishing Company, Inc., to create a series of wonderful scroll saw books. This set of books is reasonably priced in order that scrollers can compile a great collection of scroll saw patterns and projects at a minimum cost. (In most cases less than twenty five cents per pattern.)

If you purchase—and like—any one book in this set of books, you should look at other books in the series, as we think you will want the other books as well.

The following people have my gratitude for helping with this book. Without them all this book could never have been published. First of all, to my wife Joyce, who interpreted my horrible writing and poor spelling. She turned my "hen scratching" into an actual manuscript for this book. To Hilary, my ten-year-old granddaughter, for helping Joyce paint many projects. Also, to Bill Ray of Akron, Ohio, and Paul Revere of Florida for helping me make many of the projects. Alan Giagnocavo and staff at Fox Chapel Publishing Company, Inc., without their help this book could not have been published.

I would like to acknowledge and thank those of you who have purchased my book. I sincerely hope you will enjoy our efforts.

John A. Nelson
PO Box 422
Dublin, NH 03444–0422

TT186
.N434
1998x

To order your copy of this book,
please send check or money order
for $9.95 plus $2.50 shipping to:
Fox Chapel Book Orders
1970 Broad Street
East Petersburg, PA 17520

Try your favorite book supplier first!

Table of Contents

Basic Instructions

In choosing the wood, be sure to choose an interesting piece of wood, a piece of wood with character and a nice grain pattern to it. (Remember, the _wood_ is the _least_ expensive part of your project --- it is your _time_ cutting and finishing the project that is the actual "cost".)

After carefully choosing wood for your project, cut the wood to overall size.

Sand the top and bottom surfaces with medium sandpaper. Finish up with fine sandpaper.

Make a copy of the pattern at a local copy center. Enlarge or reduce as noted on the drawing.

Because of size limitations, some of the larger patterns had to be cut in half. Simply make copies full-size or enlarged as noted, and line up the two halves and glue them back together. Take care to line up all matching lines. _Note_: Glue matching letters together, i.e., "X" to "X" and "Y" to "Y", etc.

Attach the pattern to the wood by spraying the pattern with a spray adhesive. Spray the back of the paper _not_ the wood. Let the adhesive set for a minute or two then attach pattern to the wood.

If there are interior cuts, carefully drill small starter holes for the blade to fit through, in each of the interior open areas. Carefully, make all interior cuts. (A #2 or #5 skip-tooth blade is recommended.) Be sure to keep a good sharp corners as you cut. Carefully, make the final outside cut.

Finishing

Sand all over with medium than fine sandpaper. Remove all dust from your project.

If you have to stain your project, try dipping it into a large, flat pan filled with the stain. Remove project and wipe down any excessive stain. (Pour the remaining stain back into the can for later use.) After stain dries, spray with satin or gloss varnish or lacquer, as noted above.

A few projects call for a plastic mirror as a background, simply cut the plastic as you do the wood. Glue in place.

After I have finished a project, I always put a coat of paste wax on the project. This gives your project a nice finish and "feel" to it.

Note: The projects in this book illustrates only one use of each project. Do not limit yourself only to what is suggested, try enlarging or reducing each project, change or modify the designs to create your very own project. You are limited only by your own imagination, experiment - have fun with these patterns.

COW SHELF CLOCK

MAT'L.
1/4 X 4 3/8 – 6
1/2 X 1 1/2 – 4 3/8

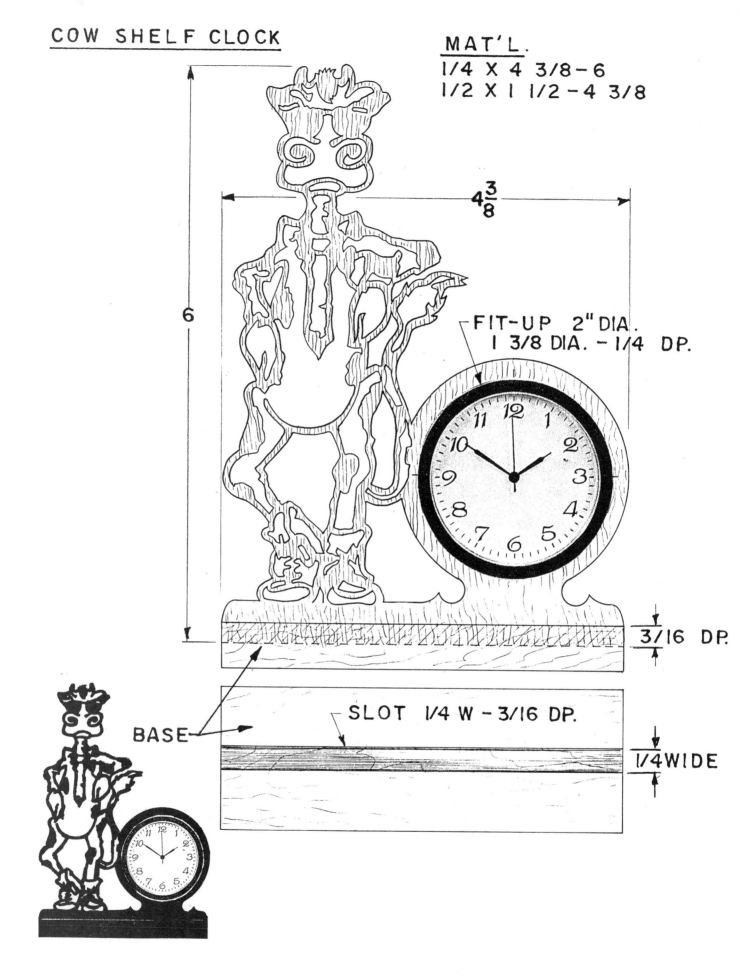

4 $\frac{3}{8}$

6

FIT-UP 2" DIA.
1 3/8 DIA. – 1/4 DP.

3/16 DP.

BASE

SLOT 1/4 W – 3/16 DP.

1/4 WIDE

LIGHTHOUSE WALL CLOCK

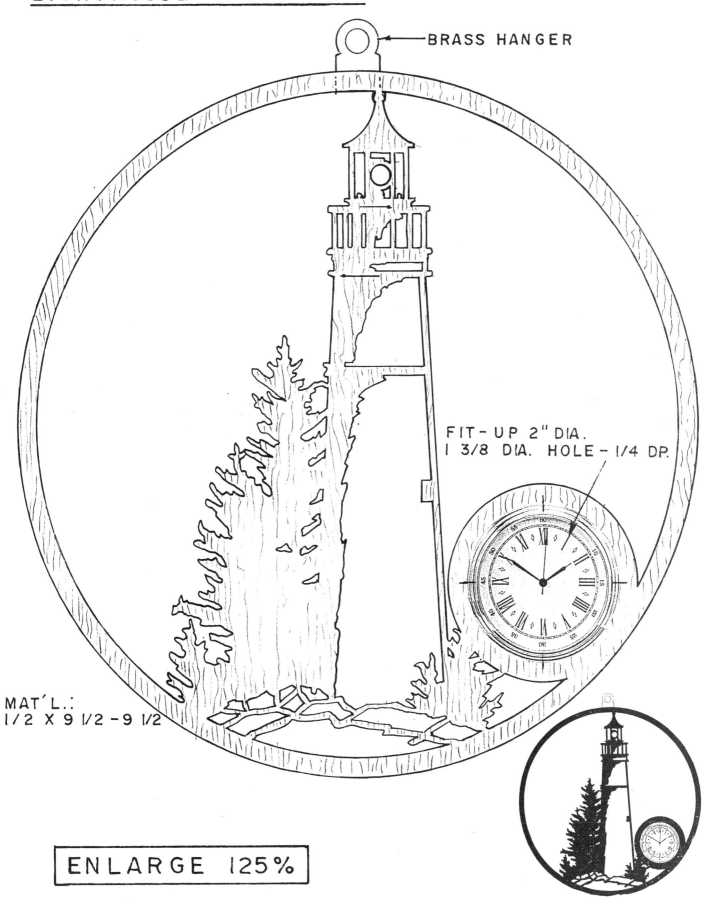

BRASS HANGER

FIT-UP 2" DIA.
I 3/8 DIA. HOLE – 1/4 DP.

MAT'L.:
1/2 X 9 1/2 – 9 1/2

ENLARGE 125%

SUPER SIMPLE Scroll Saw Clocks

3

CAT WALL CLOCK

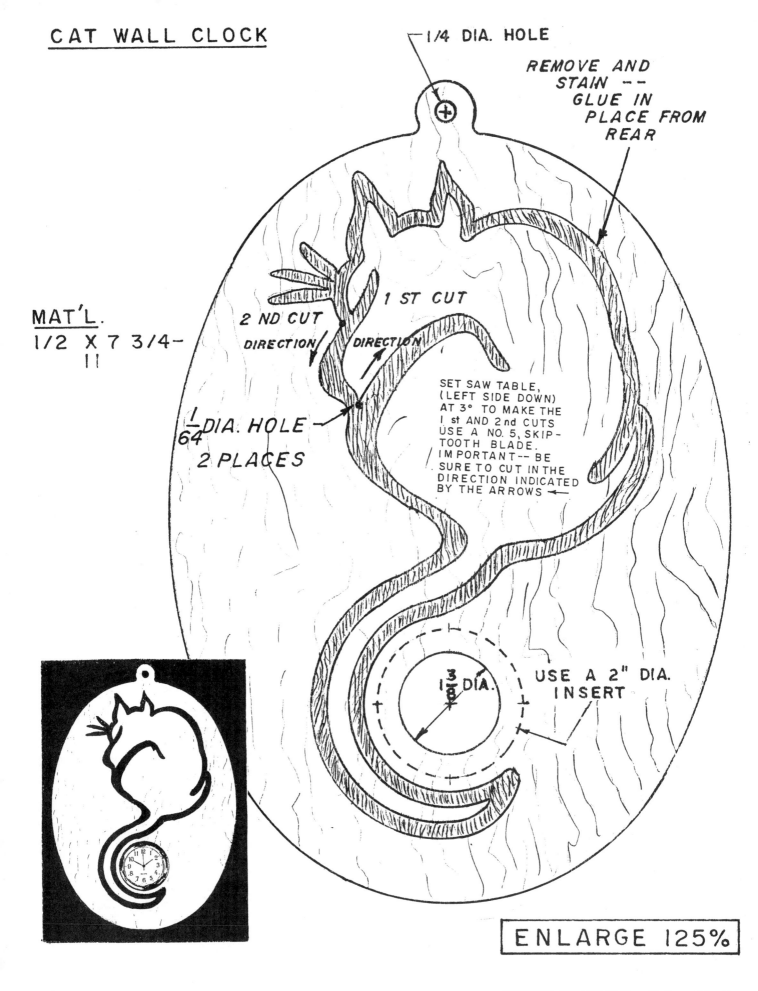

— 1/4 DIA. HOLE

REMOVE AND STAIN -- GLUE IN PLACE FROM REAR

MAT'L.
1/2 X 7 3/4 - 11

2 ND CUT DIRECTION

1 ST CUT DIRECTION

SET SAW TABLE, (LEFT SIDE DOWN) AT 3° TO MAKE THE 1 st AND 2 nd CUTS USE A NO. 5, SKIP-TOOTH BLADE. IMPORTANT -- BE SURE TO CUT IN THE DIRECTION INDICATED BY THE ARROWS ←

$\frac{1}{64}$ DIA. HOLE 2 PLACES

$1\frac{3}{8}$ DIA.

USE A 2" DIA. INSERT

ENLARGE 125%

SUPER SIMPLE Scroll Saw Clocks

SAIL BOAT WEATHER STATION

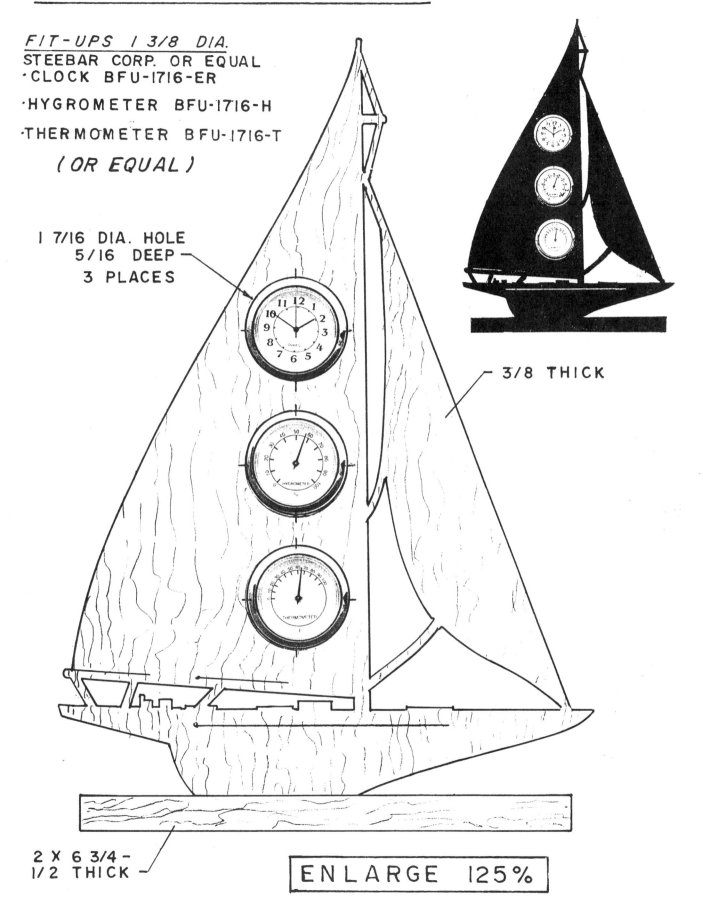

FIT-UPS 1 3/8 DIA.
STEEBAR CORP. OR EQUAL
· CLOCK BFU-1716-ER

· HYGROMETER BFU·1716·H

· THERMOMETER BFU·1716·T

(OR EQUAL)

1 7/16 DIA. HOLE
5/16 DEEP
3 PLACES

3/8 THICK

2 X 6 3/4 –
1/2 THICK

ENLARGE 125%

SCROLL SAW WALL CLOCK

1 3/8 DIA.
5/16 DP

USE A 1 7/16 DIA. FIT-UP
MAT'L. 1/2 X 10 - 10 1/2

ENLARGE 140%

FARM YARD WALL CLOCK

$2\frac{1}{8}$ DIA.

$\frac{11}{16}$ DEEP

MAT'L.:
3/4 X 10 1/4 – 10 3/4

INSERT 2 5/16 DIA.

ENLARGE 150 %

JUMPING DOLPHINS SHELF CLOCK

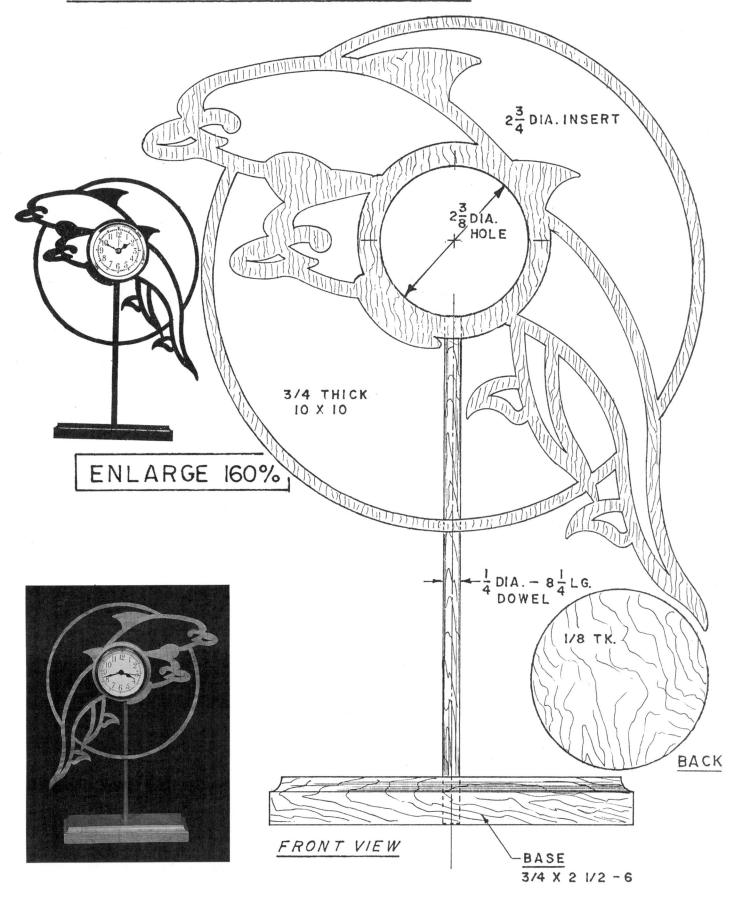

ENLARGE 160%

$2\frac{3}{4}$ DIA. INSERT

$2\frac{3}{8}$ DIA. HOLE

3/4 THICK
10 X 10

$\frac{1}{4}$ DIA. - $8\frac{1}{4}$ LG.
DOWEL

1/8 TK.

BACK

FRONT VIEW

BASE
3/4 X 2 1/2 - 6

OCTOPUS WALL CLOCK

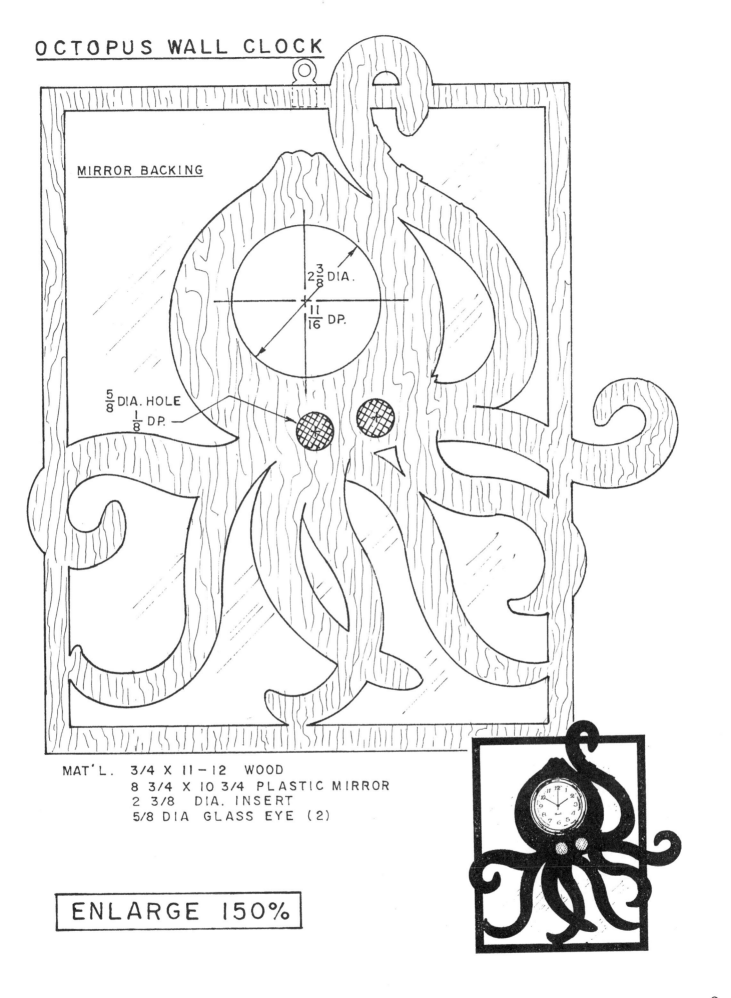

MIRROR BACKING

$2\frac{3}{8}$ DIA.

$\frac{11}{16}$ DP.

$\frac{5}{8}$ DIA. HOLE
$\frac{1}{8}$ DP.

MAT'L. 3/4 X 11-12 WOOD
8 3/4 X 10 3/4 PLASTIC MIRROR
2 3/8 DIA. INSERT
5/8 DIA GLASS EYE (2)

ENLARGE 150%

GOLDFISH WALL CLOCK AND THERMOMETER

MAT'L.
1/2 X 7 5/8 – 16 1/4

2 3/4 DIA. INSERT
2 3/4 DIA. THERMOMETER

*OPTIONAL –
BLUE PLASTIC
MIRROR*

ENLARGE
170 %

$2\frac{3}{8}$ DIA. HOLE

THERMOMETER

$2\frac{3}{8}$ DIA. HOLE

CLOCK INSERT

KITTEN WALL CLOCK

MAT'L.
1/2 X 9 –12 1/2

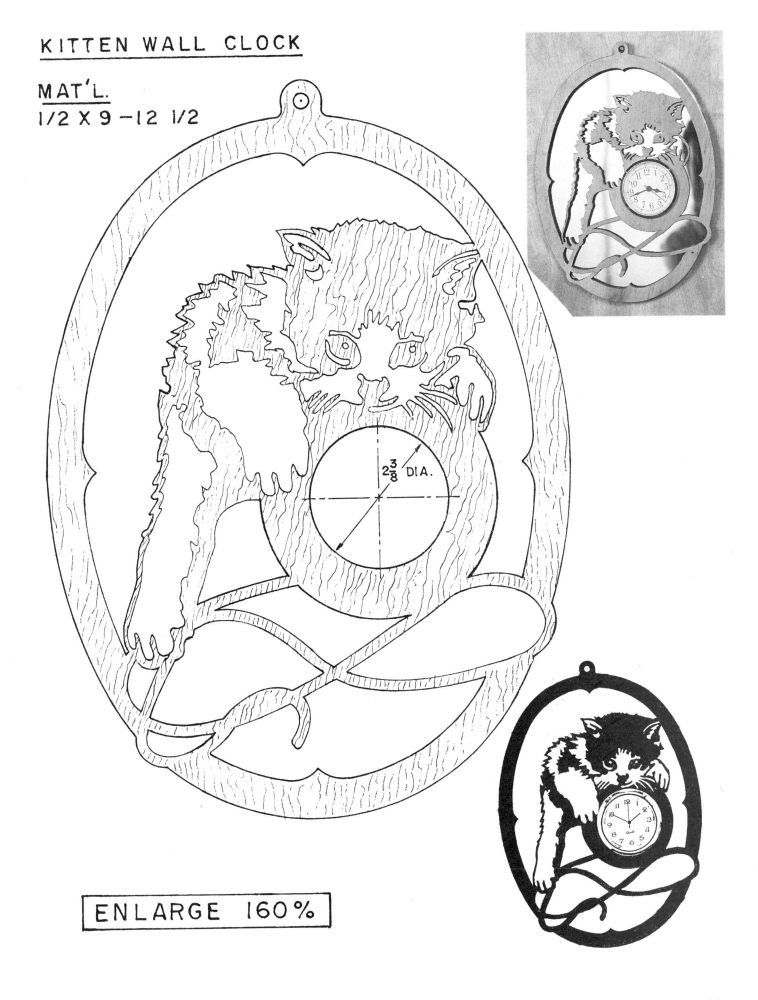

$2\frac{3}{8}$ DIA.

ENLARGE 160%

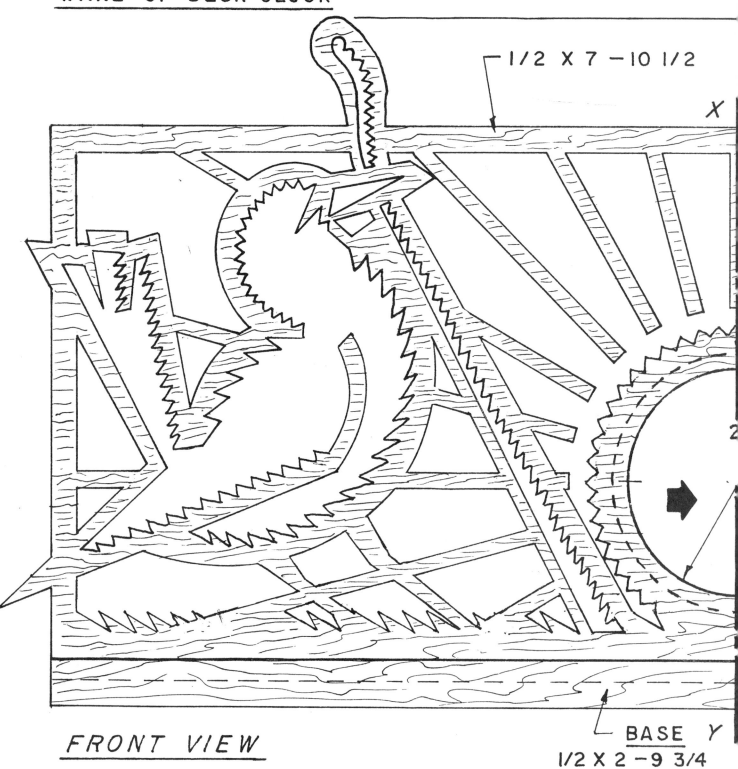

1/2 X 7 — 10 1/2

X

FRONT VIEW

BASE Y
1/2 X 2 — 9 3/4

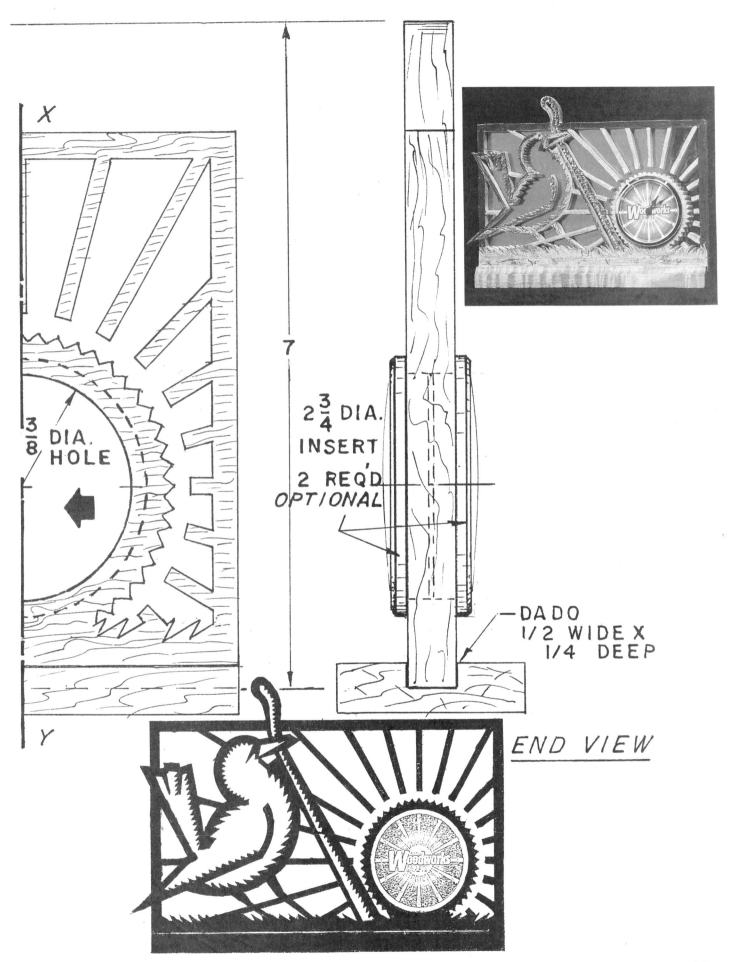

X

$\frac{3}{8}$ DIA.
HOLE

7

$2\frac{3}{4}$ DIA.
INSERT

2 REQ'D
OPTIONAL

DADO
1/2 WIDE X
1/4 DEEP

END VIEW

Y

HAPPER GOLFER
DESK CLOCK

OPTIONAL
USE A LIGHT
GREEN CLOTH
BACKING

ENLARGE
120 %

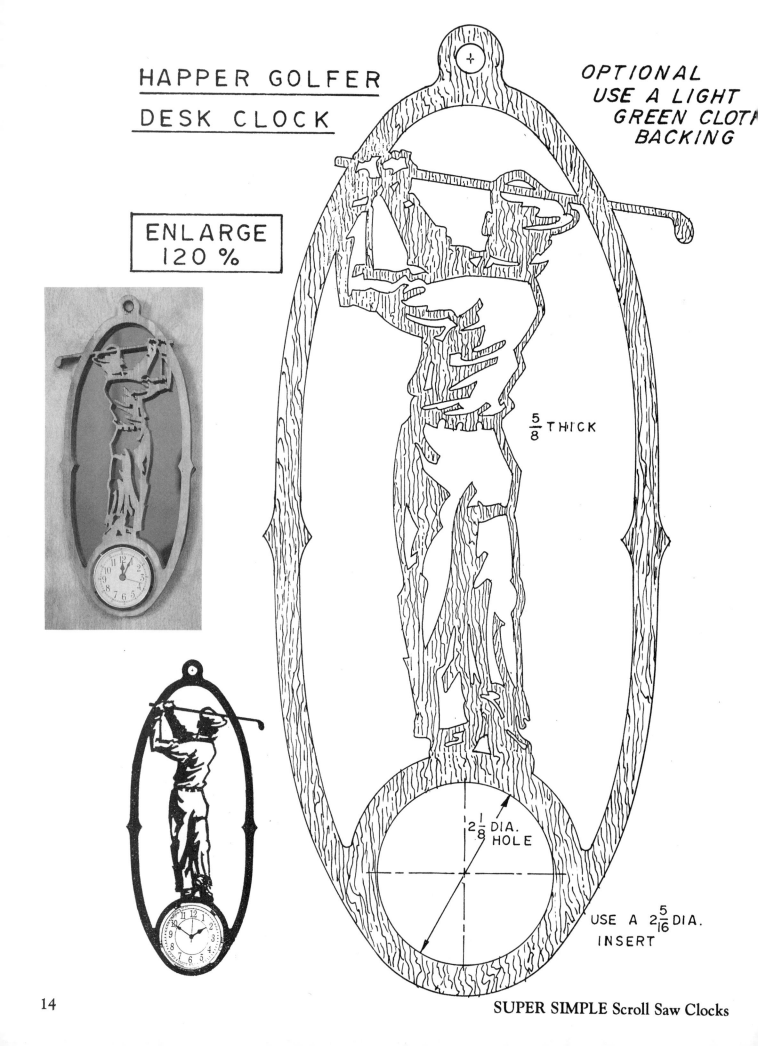

$\frac{5}{8}$ THICK

$2\frac{1}{8}$ DIA.
HOLE

USE A $2\frac{5}{16}$ DIA.
INSERT

14

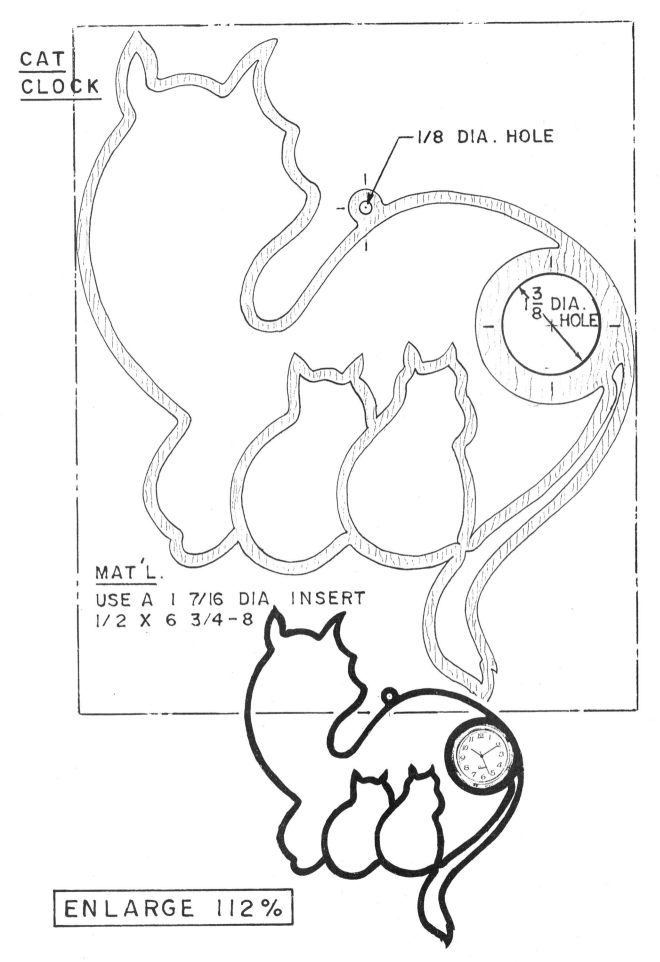

CAT
CLOCK

—1/8 DIA. HOLE

3/8 DIA. HOLE

MAT'L.
USE A 1 7/16 DIA INSERT
1/2 X 6 3/4 - 8

ENLARGE 112%

MAT'L.: 1/2 X 9 5/8 -11 1/4

FIT-UP 2" DIA.
1 3/8 DIA. HOLE-1/4 DP

X

X

Y

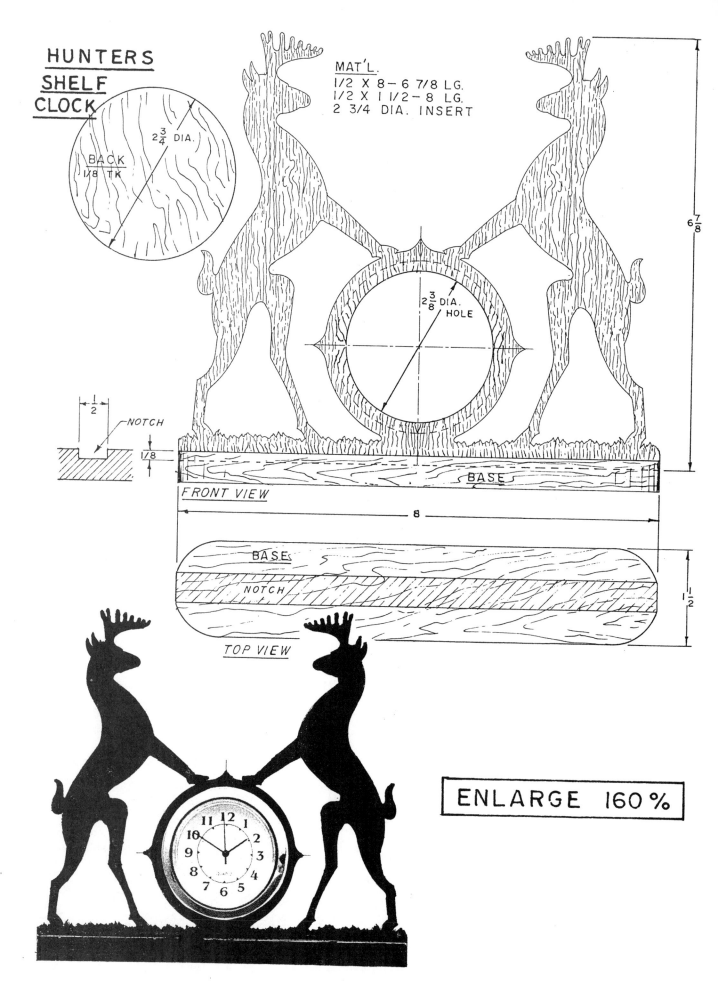

HUNTERS
SHELF
CLOCK

2 ¾ DIA.

BACK
1/8 TK

MAT'L.
1/2 X 8 — 6 7/8 LG.
1/2 X 1 1/2 — 8 LG.
2 3/4 DIA. INSERT

6 ⅞

2 ⅜ DIA.
HOLE

½

NOTCH

1/8

FRONT VIEW

BASE

8

BASE

NOTCH

1 ½

TOP VIEW

ENLARGE 160%

HUNTERS DESK CLOCK

MAT'L.
1/4 X 4 – 3 1/2
1/4 X 3/4 – 4
1 7/16 DIA. INSERT

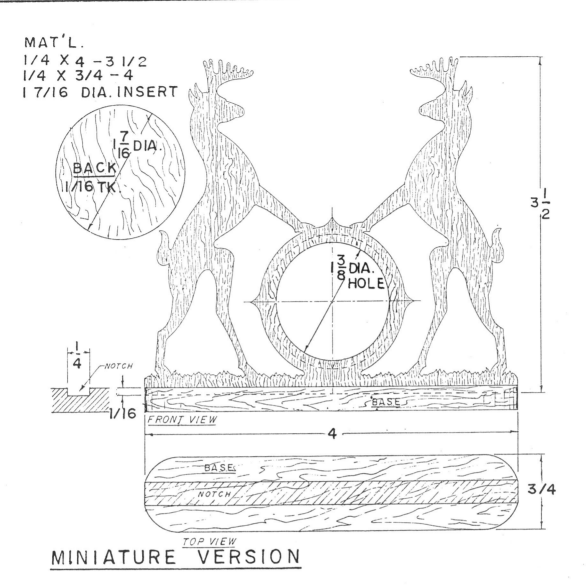

$1\frac{7}{16}$ DIA.

BACK
1/16 TK

$1\frac{3}{8}$ DIA. HOLE

$3\frac{1}{2}$

$\frac{1}{4}$

NOTCH

1/16

FRONT VIEW

BASE

4

BASE

NOTCH

TOP VIEW

3/4

MINIATURE VERSION

CARPENTERS WALL CLOCK

ENLARGE 130%

MAT'L.
1/2 X 10 - 10 3/4

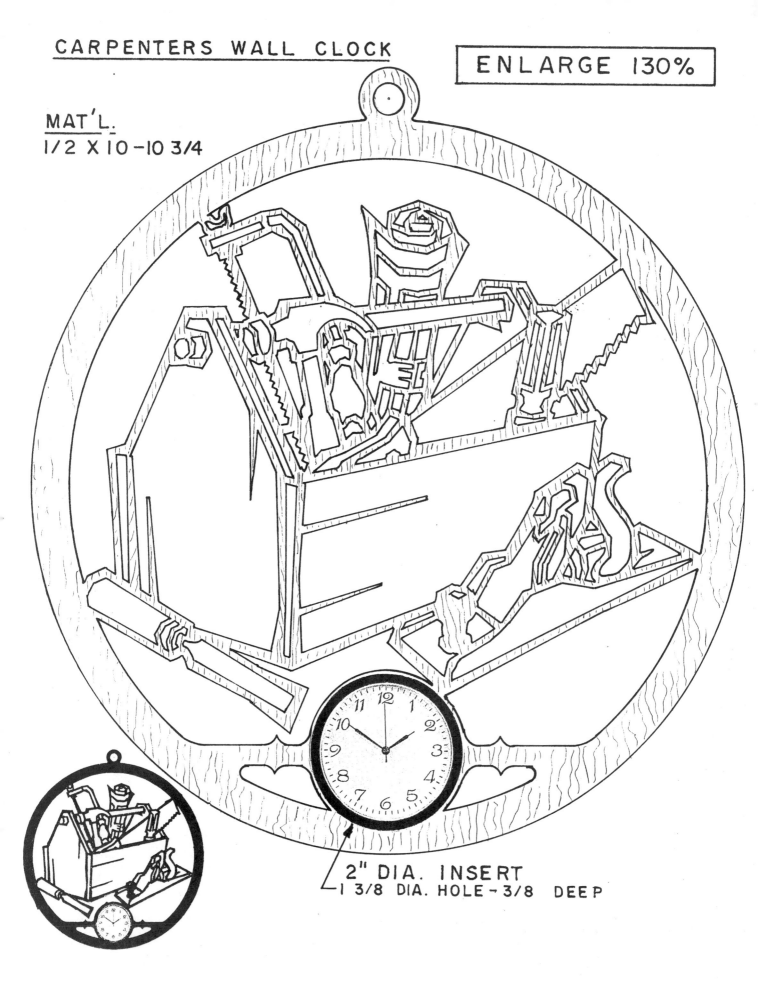

2" DIA. INSERT
— 1 3/8 DIA. HOLE - 3/8 DEEP

HUNTING WALL CLOCK

MAT'L.

1/2 X 9 3/4-10 1/2

2 3/4 DIA. INSERT

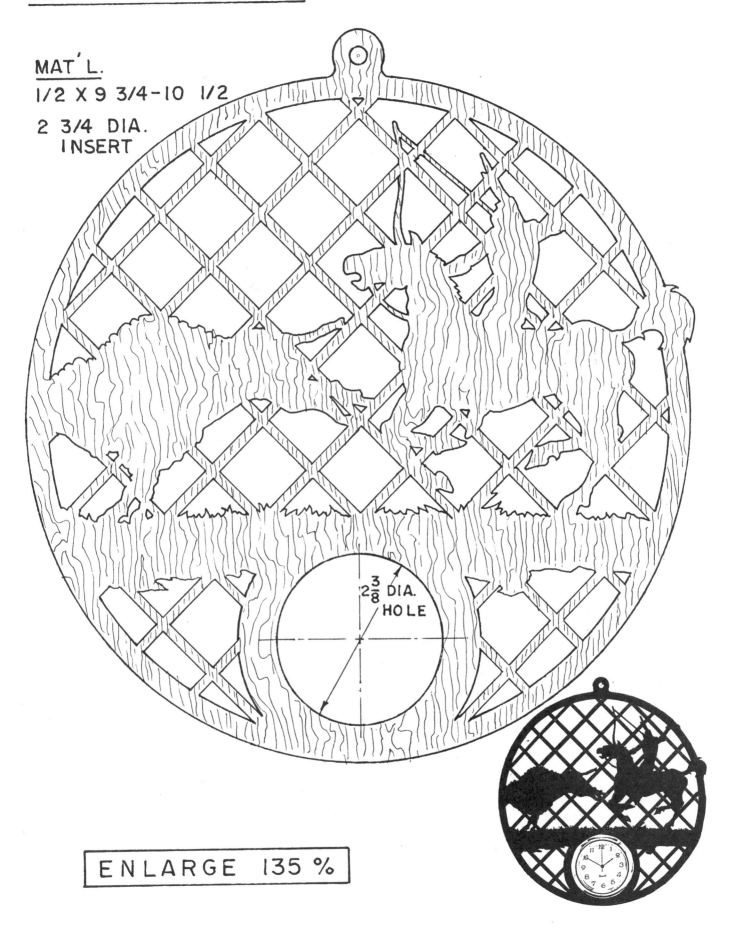

$2\frac{3}{8}$ DIA. HOLE

ENLARGE 135 %

RUNNING DEER WALL CLOCK

MAT'L
1/2 X 10-10 1/2
2 3/4 DIA.
INSERT

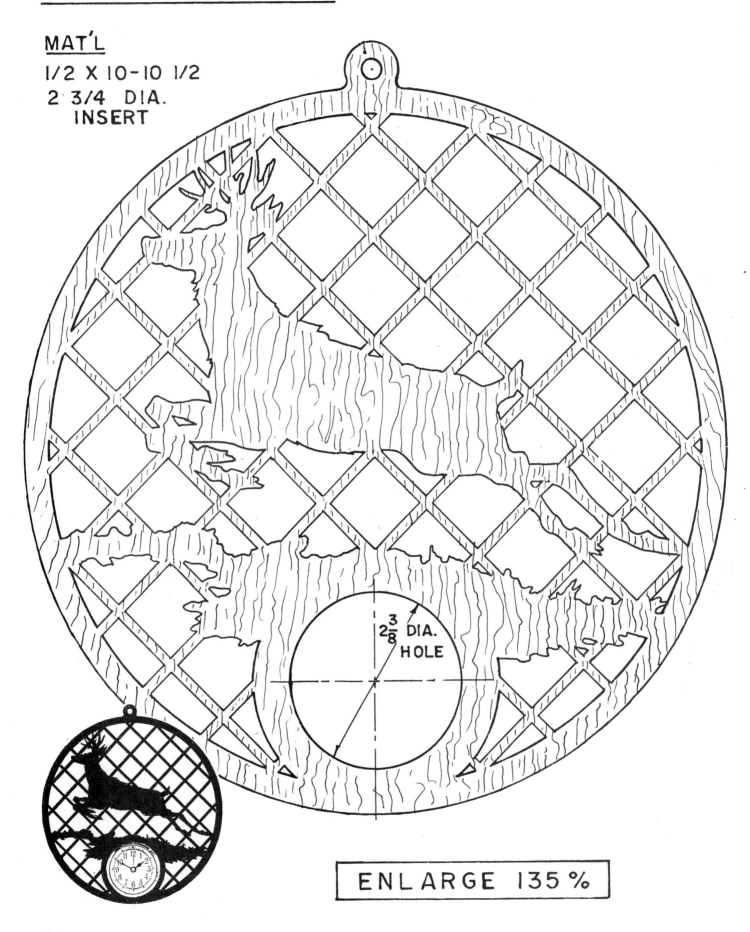

$2\frac{3}{8}$ DIA.
HOLE

ENLARGE 135%

MOOSE WALL CLOCK

MAT'L.
1/2 X 10 – 10 1/2
2 3/4 DIA.
INSERT

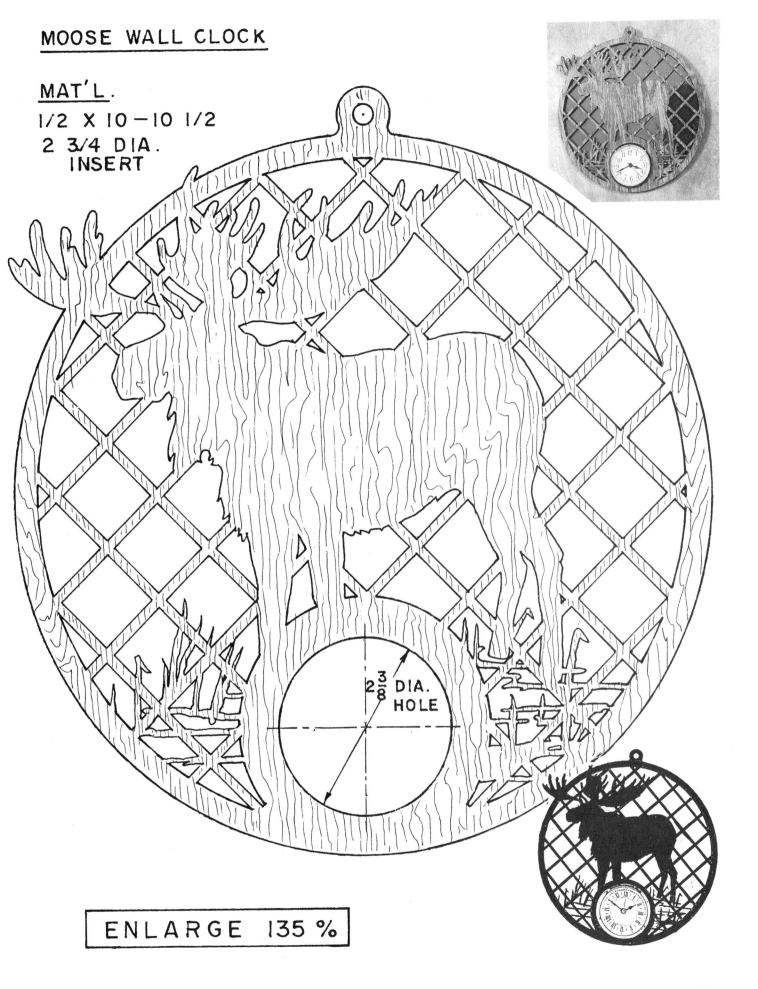

$2\frac{3}{8}$ DIA. HOLE

ENLARGE 135 %

FRONT VIEW

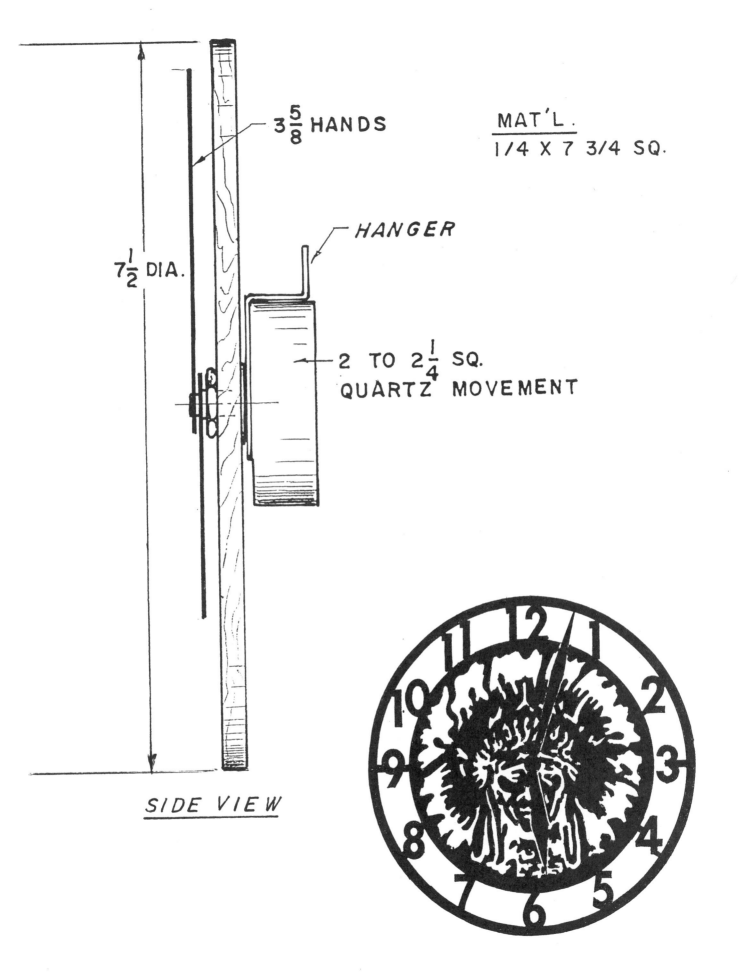

$3\frac{5}{8}$ HANDS

MAT'L.
1/4 X 7 3/4 SQ.

HANGER

$7\frac{1}{2}$ DIA.

2 TO $2\frac{1}{4}$ SQ.
QUARTZ MOVEMENT

SIDE VIEW

FRONT VIEW

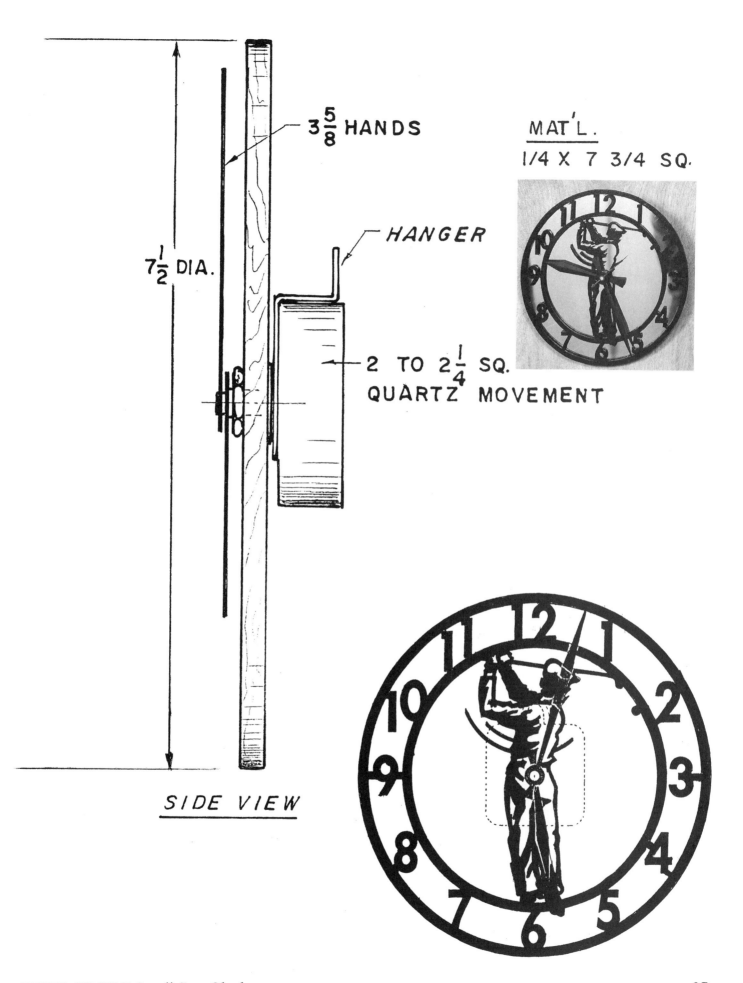

$3\frac{5}{8}$ HANDS

MAT'L.
1/4 X 7 3/4 SQ.

HANGER

$7\frac{1}{2}$ DIA.

2 TO $2\frac{1}{4}$ SQ.
QUARTZ MOVEMENT

SIDE VIEW

FRONT VIEW

SUPER SIMPLE Scroll Saw Clocks

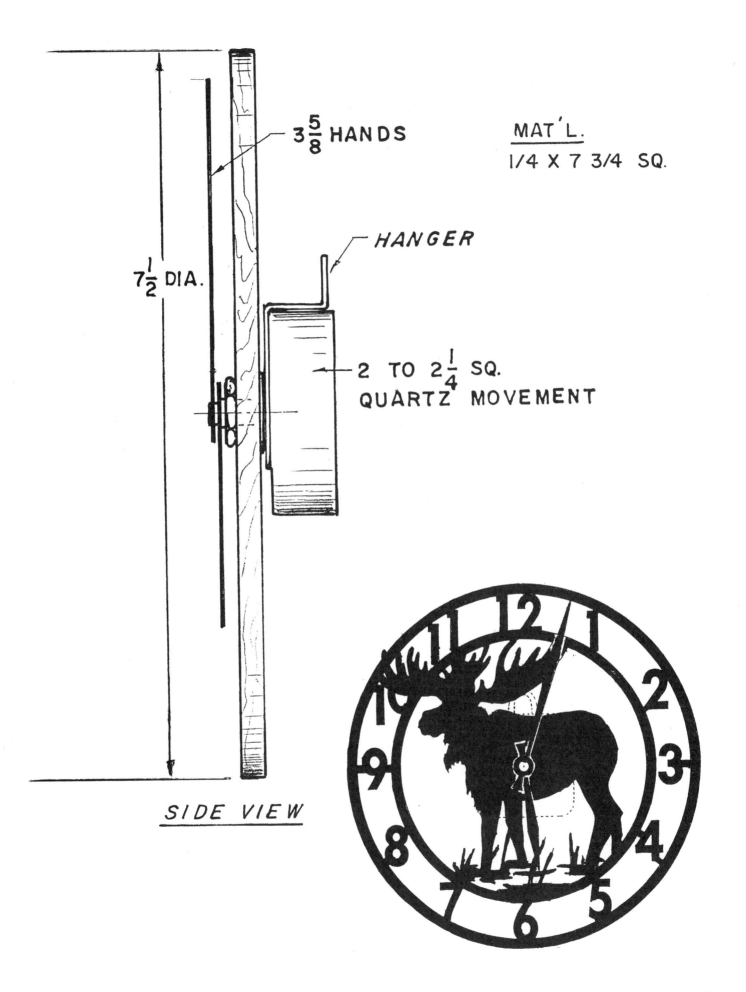

$3\frac{5}{8}$ HANDS

MAT'L.
1/4 X 7 3/4 SQ.

HANGER

$7\frac{1}{2}$ DIA.

2 TO $2\frac{1}{4}$ SQ.
QUARTZ MOVEMENT

SIDE VIEW

PUPPY LOVE WALL CLOCK
C. 1910

FRONT VIEW

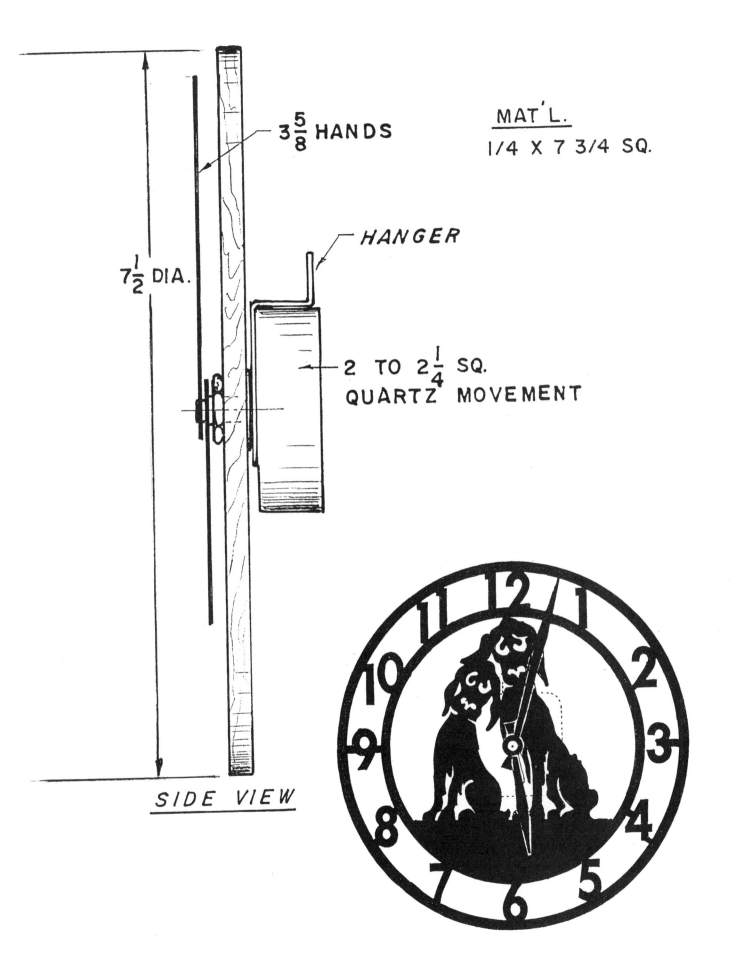

$3\frac{5}{8}$ HANDS

MAT'L.
1/4 X 7 3/4 SQ.

HANGER

$7\frac{1}{2}$ DIA.

2 TO $2\frac{1}{4}$ SQ.
QUARTZ MOVEMENT

SIDE VIEW

SUPER SIMPLE Scroll Saw Clocks

31

FRONT VIEW

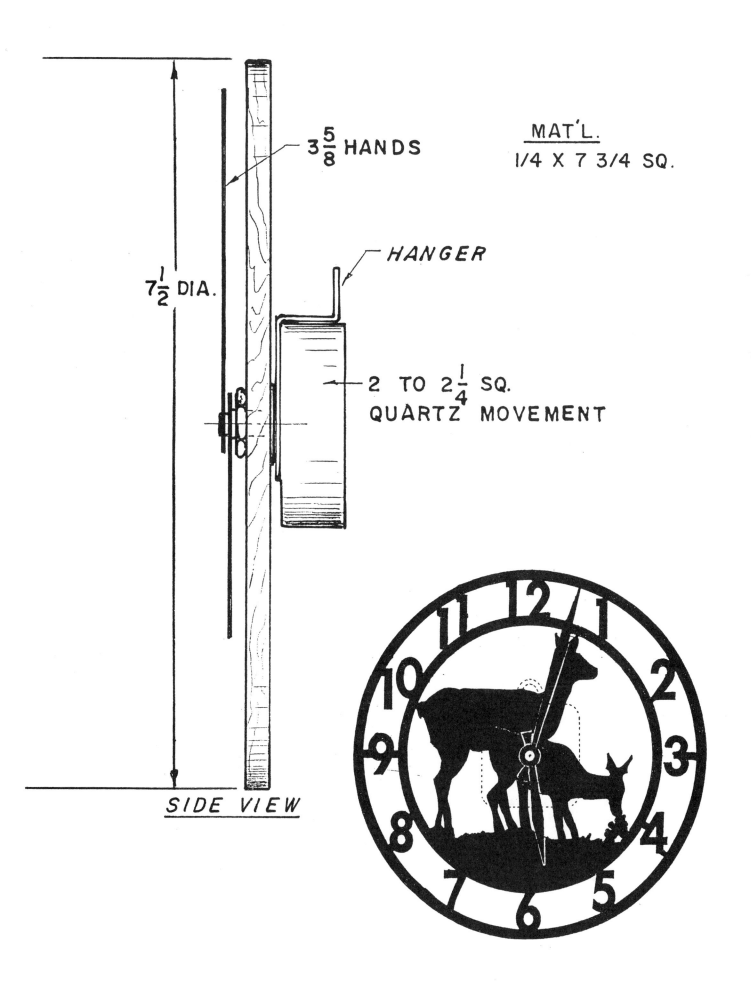

$3\frac{5}{8}$ HANDS

MAT'L.
1/4 X 7 3/4 SQ.

HANGER

$7\frac{1}{2}$ DIA.

2 TO $2\frac{1}{4}$ SQ.
QUARTZ MOVEMENT

SIDE VIEW

MAT'L : 1/2 X 8 - 9 1/4

BRASS HANGER

1 7/16 DIA. HOLE - 5/16 DP.

THERMOMETER   1 7/16 DIA.
FIT-UP CLOCK   1 7/16 DIA.

ENLARGE 125%

MAT'L: 1/2 X 8 – 9 1/4

BRASS HANGER

1 7/16 DIA. HOLE – 5/16 DP.

THERMOMETER 1 7/16 DIA.
FIT–UP CLOCK 1 7/16 DIA.

ENLARGE 125%

DEER WALL CLOCK

MAT'L: 1/2 X 10 1/2 - 11 1/4

FIT-UP 2" DIA.
1 3/8 DIA. HOLE--
1/4 DEEP

ENLARGE 160 %

INDIAN WALL CLOCK

3 1/2 DIA. INSERT
3 1/8 DIA. HOLE - 11/16 DEEP

MAT'L.:
3/4 X 10 1/2 - 15 1/2

ENLARGE 200 %

X

Y

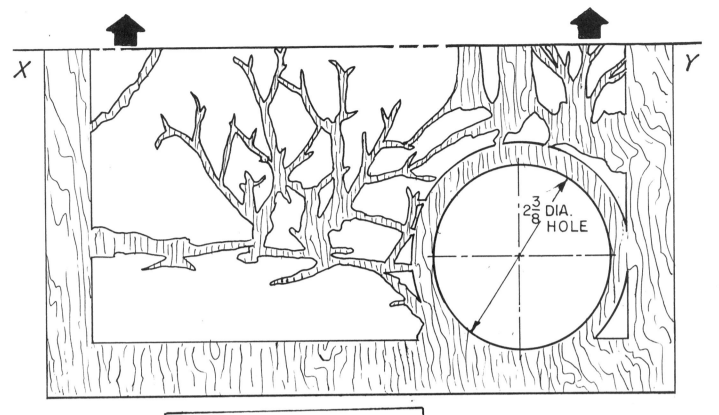

X   Y

$2\frac{3}{8}$ DIA. HOLE

ENLARGE 130 %

MAT'L.
1/2 X 8 5/8 – 15 7/8
CLOTH BACKING (*OPTIONAL*)
2 3/4 DIA. INSERT

X

$1\frac{3}{8}$ DIA.

2 DIA. FIT-UP

Y

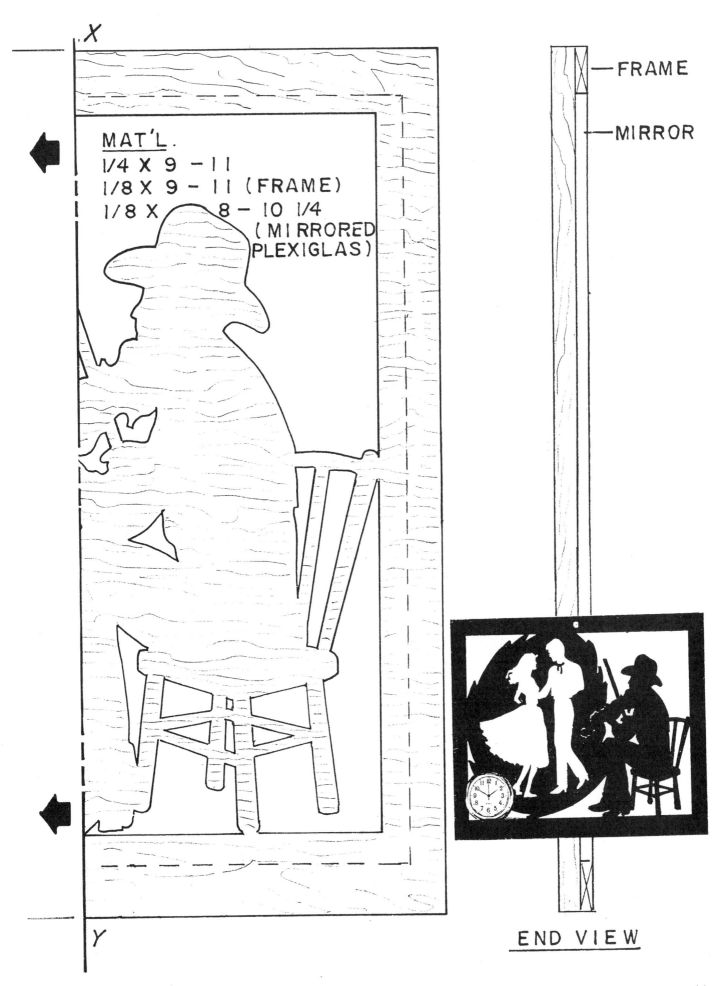

X

MAT'L.
1/4 X 9 - 11
1/8 X 9 - 11 (FRAME)
1/8 X   8 - 10 1/4
       (MIRRORED
       PLEXIGLAS)

Y

FRAME

MIRROR

END VIEW

FRIENDS WALL CLOCK

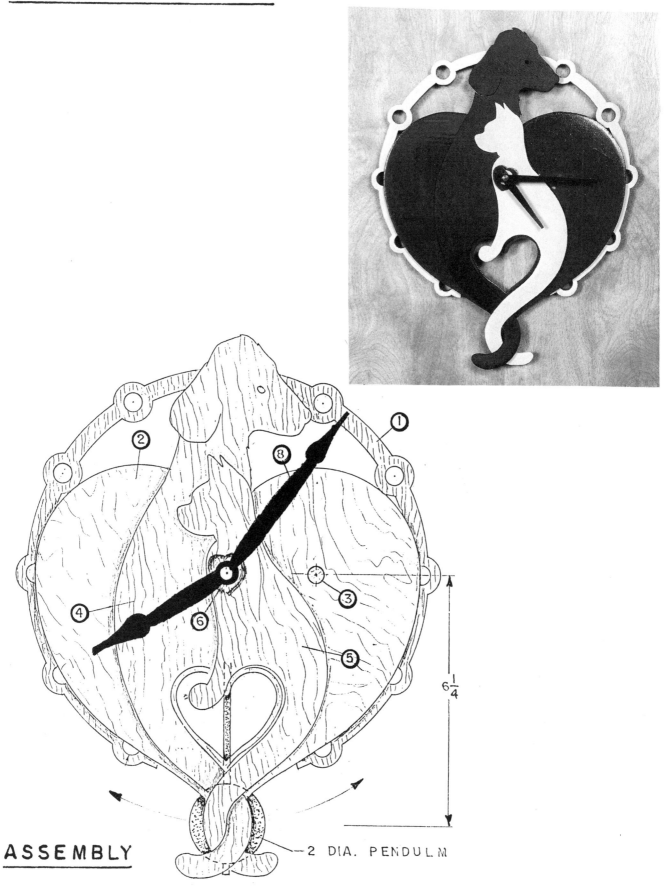

ASSEMBLY

6 1/4

—2 DIA. PENDULM

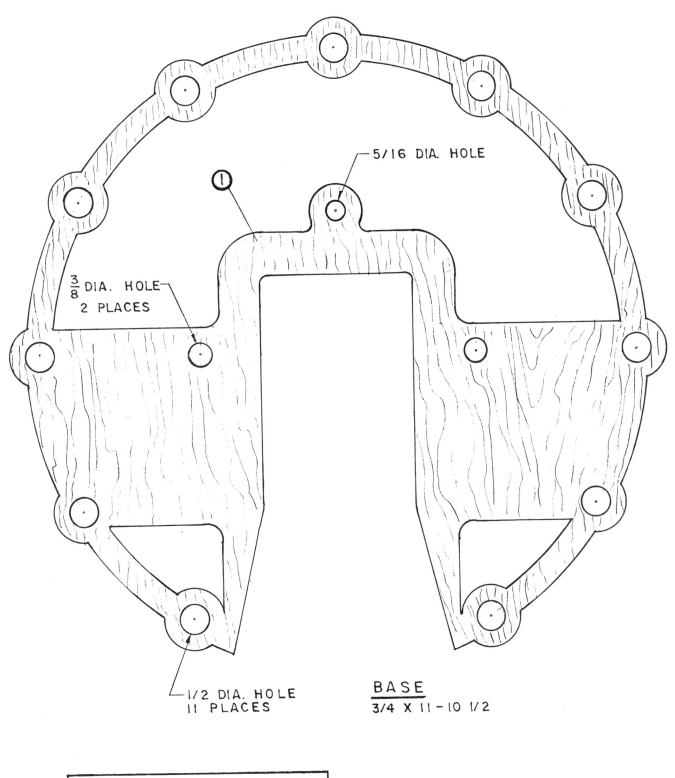

5/16 DIA. HOLE

$\frac{3}{8}$ DIA. HOLE
2 PLACES

1/2 DIA. HOLE
11 PLACES

BASE
3/4 X 11 - 10 1/2

ENLARGE 155%

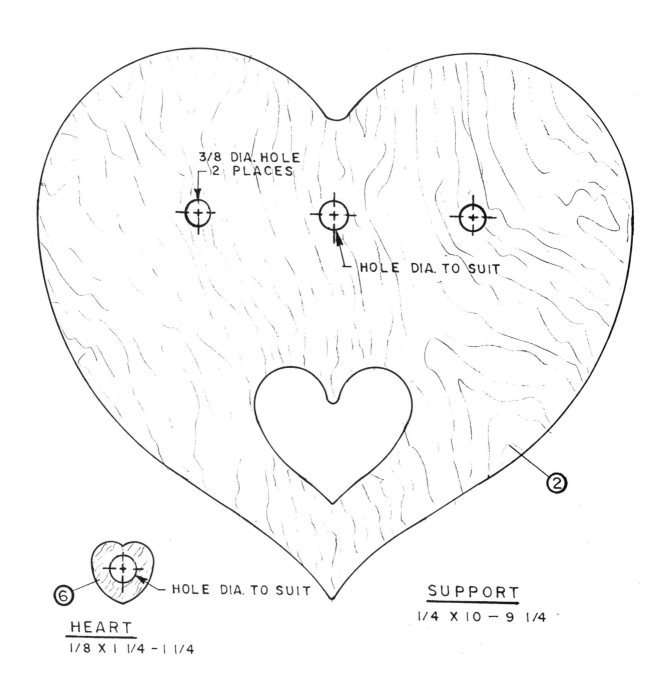

3/8 DIA. HOLE
2 PLACES

HOLE DIA. TO SUIT

②

HOLE DIA. TO SUIT

⑥

HEART
1/8 X 1 1/4 - 1 1/4

SUPPORT
1/4 X 10 — 9 1/4

ENLARGE 155%

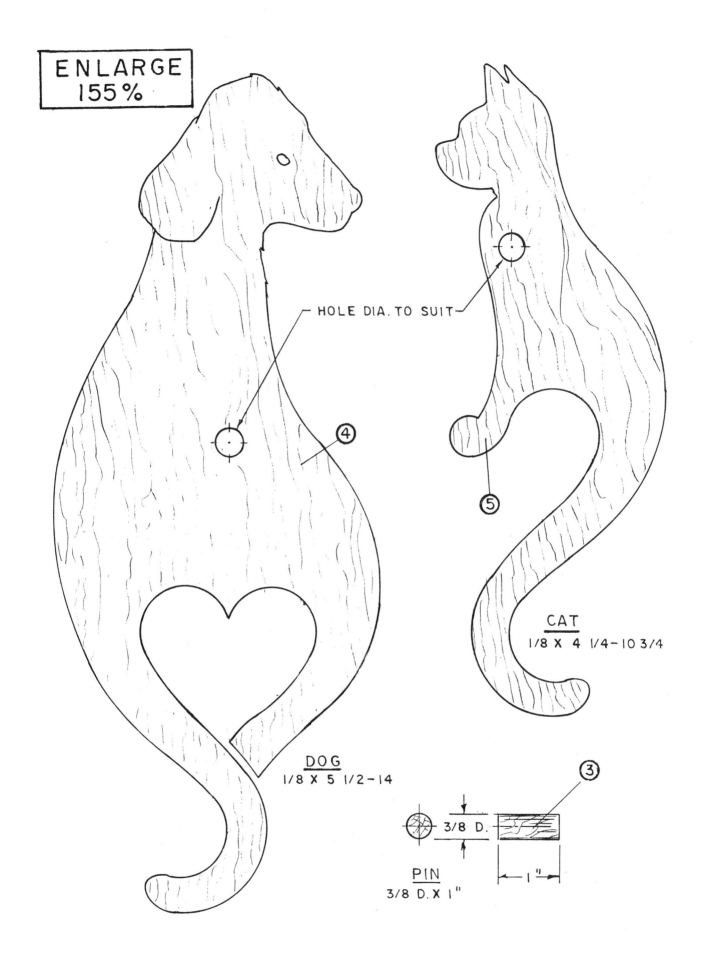

ENLARGE
155%

HOLE DIA. TO SUIT

④

⑤

CAT
1/8 X 4 1/4 — 10 3/4

DOG
1/8 X 5 1/2 — 14

③

3/8 D.

1"

PIN
3/8 D. X 1"

X

CLOCK – BFU–1716–ER
HYGROMETER BFU–1716–H
THERMOMETER BFU–1716–T
STEEBAR NOS. OR EQUAL (1 7/16 DIA.)

$1\frac{3}{8}$ DIA
CLOCK $\frac{5}{16}$ DP.

THERMOMETER HYGROME

MAT'L.
1/2 X 10 5/8 –12 7/8

Y

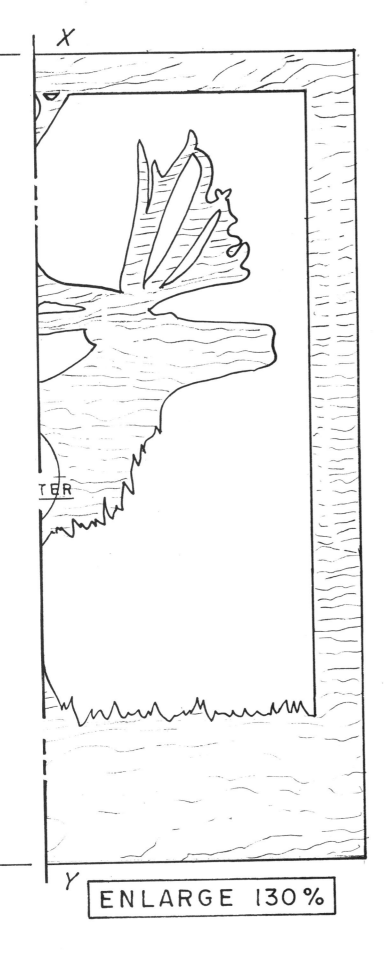

X

TER

Y

ENLARGE 130%

CHILD'S DESK CLOCK
C. 1910

MAT'L.
3/4 X 10 1/4 —
13 3/4

$2\frac{3}{4}$ DIA. INSERT

$2\frac{3}{8}$ DIA. HOLE-
THRU

ENLARGE 160%

PLEASE WILL YOU TELL ME THE RIGHT TIME

DADO
3/4 W
1/4 DP

BASE   3/4 X 2 1/2 — 10

10

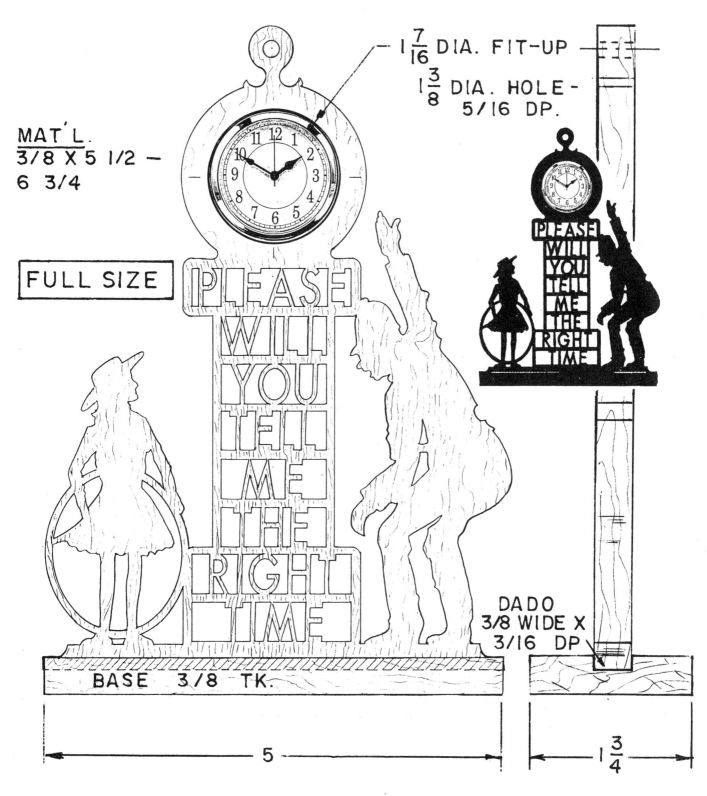

MAT'L.
3/8 X 5 1/2 —
6 3/4

FULL SIZE

$1\frac{7}{16}$ DIA. FIT-UP

$1\frac{3}{8}$ DIA. HOLE —
5/16 DP.

PLEASE WILL YOU TELL ME THE RIGHT TIME

BASE   3/8 TK.

DADO
3/8 WIDE X
3/16 DP

5

$1\frac{3}{4}$

MINIATURE VERSION

CAT AND BIRD WALL CLOCK

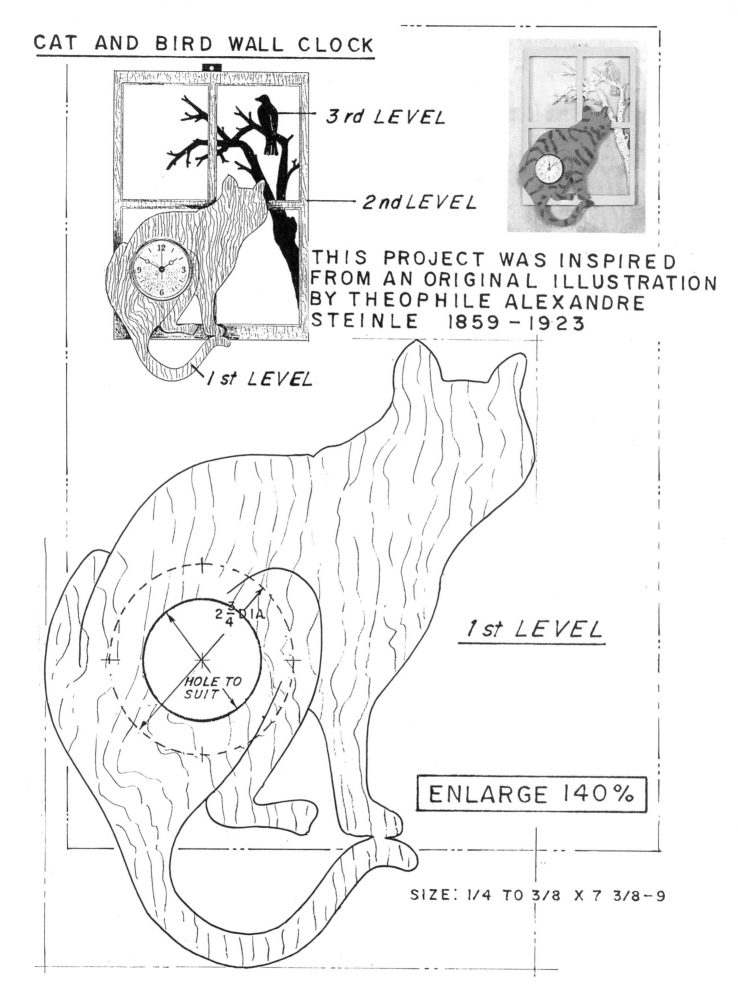

3rd LEVEL

2nd LEVEL

1st LEVEL

THIS PROJECT WAS INSPIRED
FROM AN ORIGINAL ILLUSTRATION
BY THEOPHILE ALEXANDRE
STEINLE 1859 – 1923

1st LEVEL

$2\frac{3}{4}$ DIA

HOLE TO
SUIT

ENLARGE 140%

SIZE: 1/4 TO 3/8 X 7 3/8 - 9

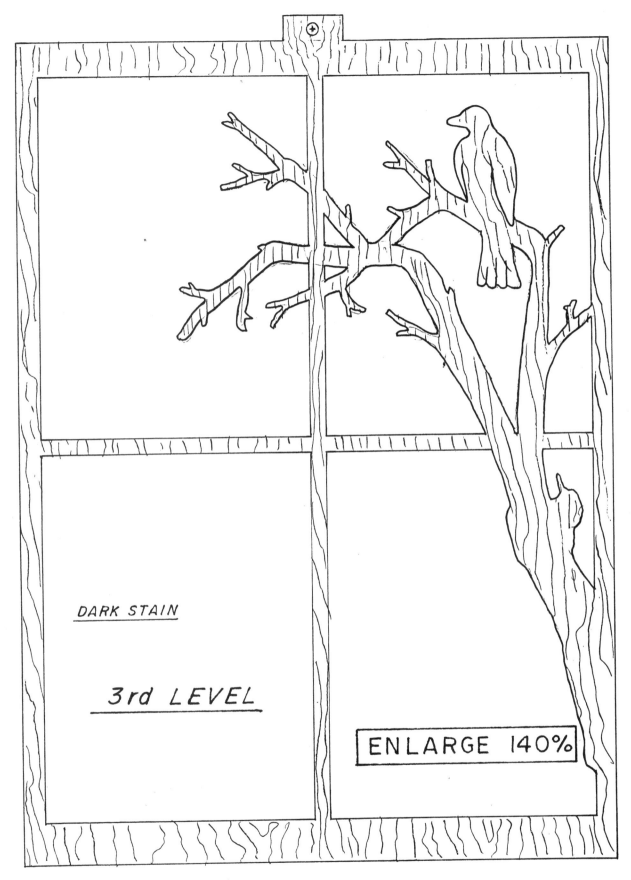

DARK STAIN

3rd LEVEL

ENLARGE 140%

SIZE: 1/4 X 8 3/4 - 12 1/4

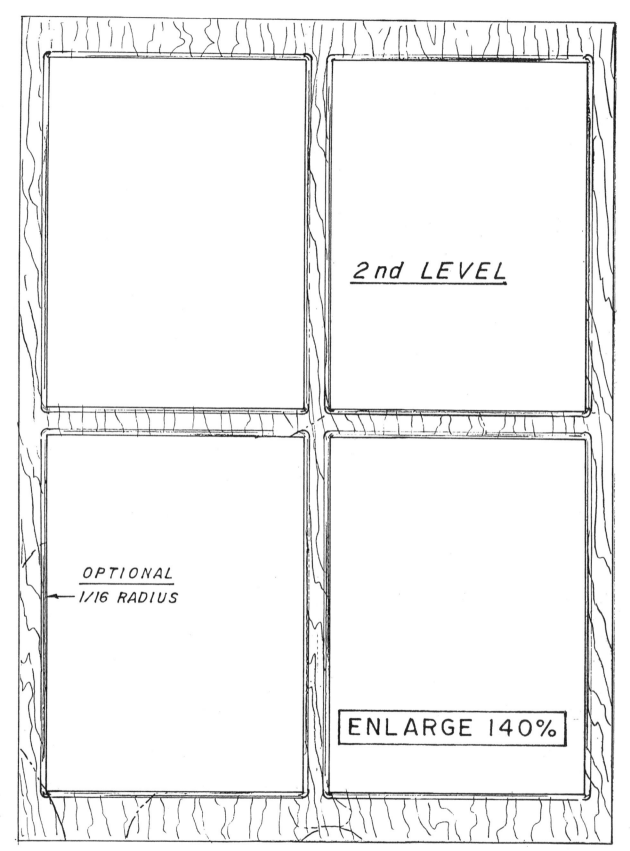

2nd LEVEL

OPTIONAL
1/16 RADIUS

ENLARGE 140%

SIZE: 1/8 X 8 3/4 — 11 7/8

FISHERMAN WALL CLOCK

ENLARGE 145%

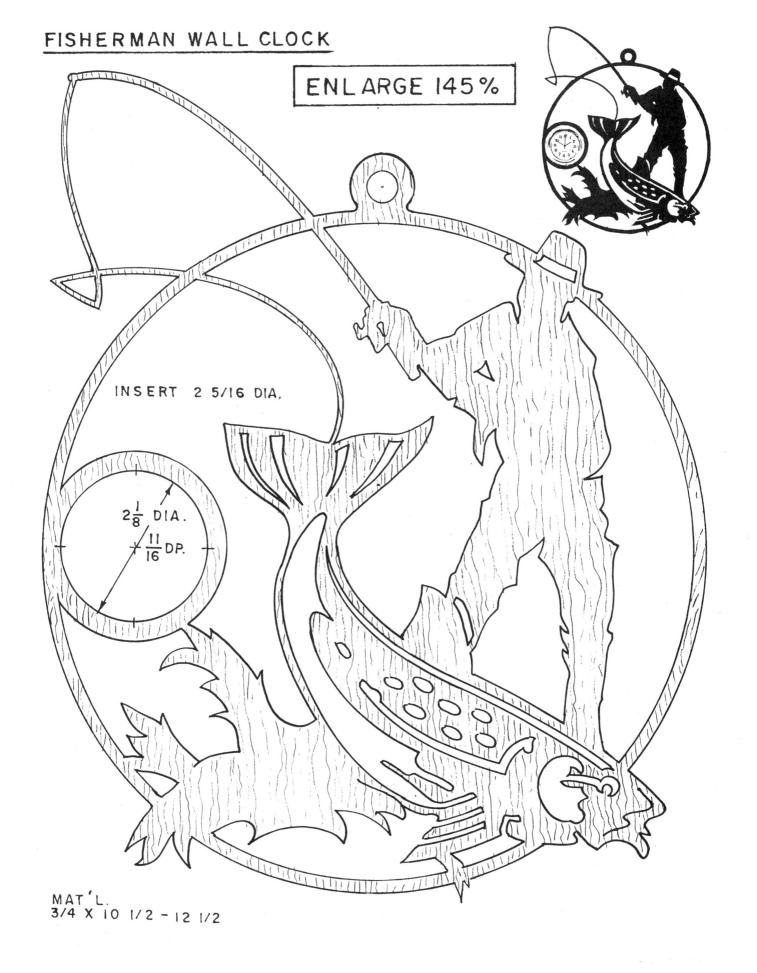

INSERT 2 5/16 DIA.

$2\frac{1}{8}$ DIA.

$\frac{11}{16}$ DP.

MAT'L.
3/4 X 10 1/2 - 12 1/2

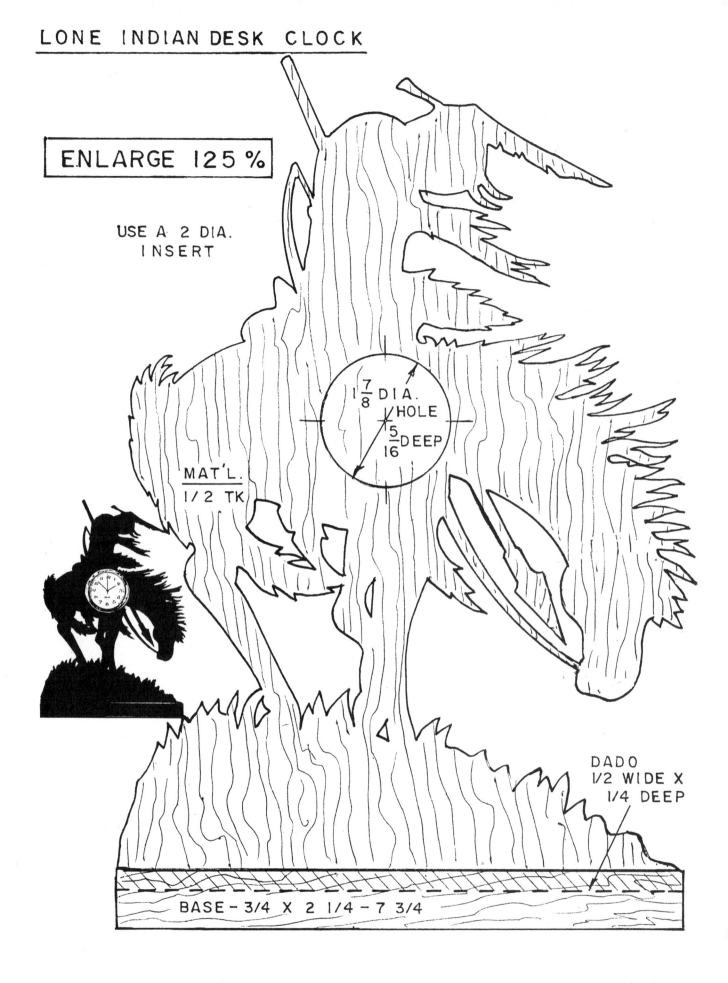

ENLARGE 125 %

USE A 2 DIA.
INSERT

$1\frac{7}{8}$ DIA.
HOLE
$\frac{5}{16}$ DEEP

MAT'L.
1/2 TK

DADO
1/2 WIDE X
1/4 DEEP

BASE - 3/4 X 2 1/4 - 7 3/4

FRIENDS DESK WEATHER STATION

1/2 X 6 3/4 – 8 3/8

$\frac{3}{8}$ DIA.

$\frac{5}{16}$ DP.

CLOCK (1 7/16) THERMOMETER HYGROMETER

BASE 3/4 X 2 1/4 – 6 3/4

1 7/16 DIA. INSERTS (3)

FARM DESK CLOCK

X

BODY
1/4 TK

$2\frac{5}{16}$ DIA. INSERT
$2\frac{1}{8}$ DIA. HOLE

a

Y

ENLARGE 130%

BRACE
1/4 TK.

UP

X

Y

Appendix 'A'

Where To Get Clock Parts and Hardware

(These are the names/addresses we know of at this time any omissions
are only because we do not know of them or simply we "goofed".) Write
them for their catalog - tell them the NELSON'S of "NELSON DESIGNS"
told you to write them.

In Alphabet Order:

Amor Crafts
PO Box 445
East Northport, NY 11731

Cherry Tree
PO Box 369
Belmont, OH 43718

Constantine
2050 Eastchester Road
Bronx, NY 10461

Don Jer Products (Suede-Tex-only)
8 Ilene Court
Belle Mead, NJ 08502

Innovation Specialties
11869 Teale Street
Culver City, CA 90230

Klockit
PO Box 636
Lake Geneva, WI 53145

Leichtung Workshops
1 Woodworkers Way
Seabrook, NH 03874

Meisel Hardware Specialties
PO Box 70
Mound, MN 55364-0070

Merritt Antiques, Inc.
RD 2
Douglasville, PA 19518

Precision Movements
4251 Chestnut Street PO Box 689
Emmaus, PA 18049-0689

P.S. Wood
10 Dowing Street Suite #3
Library, PA 15129

S. LaRose, Inc.
234 Commerce Place
Greensborough, NC 27420

Shipley Co.
2075 S. University Blvd. Suite 119
Denver, CO 80210

Sloan's Woodshop
3453 Callis Road
Lebanon, TN 37090

Steebar Corp.
PO Box 980
Andover, NJ 07821-0980

Turncraft
PO Box 70
Mound, TN 55364-0070

Woodcraft
PO Box 4000 41 Atlantic Ave.
Woburn, MA 01888

Woodworkers Supply of New Mexico
5604 Alameda NE
Albuquerque, NM 87113

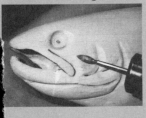